# THE
# REAL McCOY

## An A-Z of Black People in Science and Technology

D1492795

**Cover illustration: Cowings, McCoy and Egyptians**

Special thanks to Richard Gray
for his hard work and commitment

## Introduction

This series of books
is called "Black Makers of History".
We have taken great care
to base the information in them on fact.

Our work in writing them
has uncovered many things
done by Africans,
both in and out of Africa,
in all areas of life —
from Religion to Rockets to Reggae.
The first book is called "Four Women"
and the third is about
contributors to the Arts.
This second book is called "The Real McCoy".

We have used this title
because McCoy was a Black inventor
whose products were so good
that people wanted only them —
The Real McCoy, the real thing.

While doing our research, we found
that many Black inventors were not given
full credit for their work.
This includes slaves,
who were not allowed to register
their own inventions.
So it follows that many Black inventors
were not even paid
for their inventions.

Looking further back in history,
the Egyptians helped
to lay the foundations
of the Science and Technology
which we have today.

We all owe a lot to them.

Most of us have seen statues
and drawings of these Ancient Egyptians —
but have we noticed their African faces?
It is not only their faces
which tell us they were Black.

There is also evidence from tests
on the bones and skin of mummies,
from blood tests, eye-witness reports,
language and cultural clues
and what the Egyptians themselves
had to say.

They called their country "Kemet",
which means "Black Land".
The Ancient Greeks, too, made the point.
Herodotus, an Ancient Greek often called
"The Father of History",
went to Egypt.
He wrote this about the Egyptians:
"... They are black skinned
and have woolly hair."

The Black civilisation of Egypt
had close links
with other parts of Africa
and, as C.A. Diop states:
"The history of Black Africa
will remain suspended in air
and cannot be written correctly
until African historians
dare to connect it
with the history of Egypt..."

## Aircraft Design

Christine Darden is one of many
Black engineers working with NASA.
She is working on faster-than-sound flight.
At present, supersonic Concorde
can fly to New York from London
in four hours.
Christine Darden is designing aircraft
that will make the trip
in just one hour — without a sonic boom!

A

## Ancient Medicine

In ancient times,
as long as four thousand years ago,
the Egyptians gained world fame
for their medical knowledge.
Nobles from Syria and Greece
came to their hospitals
and Egyptian doctors
were given jobs abroad
by the Persians and Greeks.

Egyptian doctors
wrote on such subjects as
the body, women's health,
stomach and muscular complaints.
They had a range of surgical instruments
and were the first to do
cataract eye operations,
brain surgery and setting broken bones.

## Banneker (1731-1806)

Benjamin Banneker was able to go to school
only because his parents had bought their way
out of slavery.
This was lucky for America,
as we shall see.

Banneker was very good at Maths
and used it in very practical ways.
For example, in 1793 he wrote
the first science book by a Black American —
"Banneker's Almanac".
It gave details of sunrise and sunset,
the movement of the moon, planets and stars,
and other scientific facts.

B

Earlier, in 1789, he had predicted
the eclipse of the sun.
He also made the first clock
to be made in America.
This clock, made from wood,
kept perfect time for twenty years.

Banneker also saved farmers millions of dollars.
Their crops were often destroyed by locusts.
But Banneker worked out
that locusts came every seventeen years.
So, thanks to him, farmers knew
when the locusts would come
and could plan for it.

Banneker is best known for his part
in planning the layout of Washington, D.C.,
the capital of America.
Disaster struck when the chief planner
returned to France after a row,
taking all the plans with him.
But, lucky for America,
Banneker was able to draw them again —
from memory.

He even chose the site for the White House.
In 1791, he wrote a famous letter
to the President of the USA:
''However variable we may be
in society or religion,
however diversified
in situation or colour,
we are all in the same family
and stand in the same relation to God.''

But for luck, this man
would have been a slave.

Carver page 18

## Caesarian Section

In 1879, in a village in Uganda,
a Scottish explorer saw
a Caesarian operation.
To him it was a scientific miracle.
Scotland did not have
this medical knowledge.
He wrote that the patient was given
banana wine to ease the pain.
She was then tied to a bed
and held down by one of the surgeons.
Banana wine was also used as an antiseptic
for washing the surgeon's hands,
washing the surgical instruments
and cleaning the wound.
The incision was made with a sharp knife
and hot irons were used to stop the bleeding.

C

Every effort was made to save
both mother and child,
but if a choice had to be made,
the mother was always saved, he was told.

After the operation, seven spikes were used
to join the cut together.
In the operation he saw,
both mother and baby survived
and all was well.
The explorer stressed that
this operation was not unusual.
To the people of the village,
Caesarian operations were something
which had been going on for years.

C

## Calendar

We have the Ancient Egyptians to thank for
the three hundred and sixty-five day calendar.
They worked out the number of days
using maths and astrology.
Over six thousand years ago,
they worked it out to the exact
three hundred and sixty-five and a quarter days
which we use today.

C

## Carver (1864-1943)

George Washington Carver was
a truly remarkable man.
Born a slave,
he gave economic freedom
to farmers in the South of the USA.

When he was still a boy,
Carver was kidnapped by slave thieves.
A horse was paid for his ransom.
As a young man,
he was eager for education.
When slavery was over,
he was able to work
to pay for his education.
He was the first Black student
at his college in Iowa.
He was awarded a Master's Degree in 1896
and moved to Alabama.

Carver produced rich harvests
from a ''useless'' plot of land.
This is how he got farmers
to change from cotton farming
to peanut and sweet potato farming.
(Jimmy Carter should be grateful for this!)
This change was so successful
that there was soon more peanut
and sweet potato than was needed.

But then Carver found over
three hundred other ways
of using these foods.
From peanuts, he made
coffee, milk, cheese, flour,
soap, ink and many other things.
From sweet potatoes, he made
flour, rubber, vinegar,
molasses and many more products.

C

He was so good at finding
new ways to make familiar things
that he even made artificial marble
from wood shavings.
Another success was to find
many new uses for soya.

Carver truly worked miracles.
He was given the Roosevelt Medal in 1939.
He never tried to make money
from his inventions.
In his own words:
"What God has given me,
I have no right to sell."

C

## Cowings

Dr Patricia Cowings has worked
in many fields of space medicine research.
She was the chief investigator
in an experiment at the Space Lab Centre
in Houston, Texas.
Her work helps astronauts
to avoid space sickness and
keep fit when they are weightless.

Our bodies are made
to work in Earth's gravity.
Since there is no gravity in space,
you have to do special exercises
to keep your body as fit and healthy
in space as on earth.

C

These exercises are different for each person.
Muscles and joints have to be kept working,
blood pressure and heart-rate
have to be controlled.

Thanks to the work of scientists
like Dr Cowings,
astronauts can perform normal activities
that we take for granted,
like walking or standing,
when they return to earth.

## Diop (1923-1985)

Professor Cheik Anta Diop
was born in Senegal, West Africa.
He studied in Paris.
During his studies,
he began to find out
the positive role played by Black people
in world history.
For instance, he found evidence
that the great Egyptians
were in fact Black people.
This evidence came from
drawings, writings, statues,
skin tests, blood groupings and languages.
Yet this fact was being denied.

D

He began to write books
which were attacked
by people who should have known better.
But he answered his critics with logic
and continued to spread the news
with books, lecture tours
and at university in Senegal.
Through his efforts,
many more people now know
that civilisation owes a great deal
to Black Africa.
We also know that many of
the great pioneers of science were African.

## Dogon

The Dogon people live in Mali, West Africa.
Mali was one of
the three great empires of West Africa.

In 1931, two French scientists
went to live with the Dogon.
Sixteen years later, the Dogon
began to reveal their secret knowledge
about the stars and planets.

The Dogon people knew about
the rings of Saturn,
the moons of Jupiter
and that the Earth's moon was
"dry and dead, like dried blood."

**D**

It was a surprise to the Europeans
that these co-called ''primitive people''
had such scientific knowledge.
But what really shocked them
was that the Dogon also knew
of a star called ''Sirius B'',
because this star cannot be seen
with the naked eye.

The Dogon knew more about
the movement of this invisible star
than Western scientists.
What was more,
Dogon scientists had known about it
for seven hundred years.
Western scientists had ''discovered'' Sirius B
only in the 1890's.

D

## Drew 1904-1950)

Dr. Charles Drew is known as
"The Father Of The Blood Bank".
His work on ways of storing blood
has saved millions of lives.

He was born on 3 June, 1904,
in Washington, D.C.
At High School and College, he won awards
for his football, basketball, baseball
and track skills.
But his heart was set on a medical career.
Money was always a problem
but he went on to become a leading surgeon.

D

Dr Drew was in charge of the
"Blood For Britain" project
that saved so many lives during the "Blitz".
He was also in charge
of the blood donor project in the U.S.A.
(In spite of this, the Armed Forces asked
for "coloured" blood to be kept separate
from "white" blood.)

During his short life, Drew's main interest
was the training of Black surgeons
at the Freedmen's Hospital.
He died in a car crash in 1950
while taking three of his staff to a clinic.

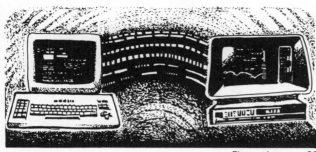

Electronics page 32

E

## Egyptians

There is a lot of evidence to show
that the Ancient Egyptians were Black —
true Africans, not Asians or Europeans.*
Five thousand years ago
Egypt was a world leader
in the things which most people
think of as "Civilisation".
The Egyptians studied many subjects,
such as philosophy, music,
art, maths, religion and science.
Egypt was a united country
with a head of state
called the Pharaoh.

*See Introduction, page 5

E

The Pharaoh also had a prime minister,
known as a "vizier".
Also, there was an upper White House
and a lower Red House of State.

At the same time
there is no record
of any signs of civilisation
in the British Isles.
It was only much later
that much knowledge passed from Africa
to the rest of the world.

E

A lot of knowledge
came to Europe from Africa
via the Ancient Greeks,
who wrote about
what they had learned
from the Egyptians.

The national hero of Ancient Egypt
was the great Imhotep.
Imhotep was a multi-genius.
He was Pharaoh Zoser's vizier.
We have him and other Egyptians
to thank for many things.
For more about Ancient Egypt,
see under A, C, F, I, K, L, P, S, U, X and Z.

E

## Electronics

Electronics is a new area of science
which started less than a hundred years ago.
Right from the start, Black people
have played an important part
and, often without any training,
have become experts in electronics.
Frederick Jones* is an early example.

Electronics plays a part
in almost every area of our lives —
tiny heart pacemakers and hearing-aids,
TV, music, cars, farming,
computers, spacecraft.

*Jones: see under J

We have room here
for only a few of the Black people
involved in electronics today.

Earl Jones' work makes it possible
for us to use small computers (at home)
to "talk" to larger computers (at work).

James West is part of the team
that invented "Foil Electrets".
These are used as tiny mikes
in hearing aids and tape recorders,
or clipped to the clothing of TV presenters.
Foil electrets are also used in hospitals,
to check heartbeat and blood pressure.

E

Brian Jackson has built computers
that can make other computers.
He has also taught a computer to see
more than the human eye can see.

Forgotten Inventors page 36

## Farming

The Ancient Egyptians were very good at farming.
They made use of many types of tool
still well-known to us today.
For example, they used a hoe
to break the ground
and a sickle to cut the crops.

When their corn was harvested
it was stored in built-in granaries.
Some were round
and some were square.
With both types of granary
the corn was poured in through the top
and taken from a small door
at the bottom.

F

## Forgotten Inventors

Have you ever wondered
who invented everyday things?
Many were invented in America
in the last century
and the early years of this one,
when the USA was becoming
a great industrial power.

And if you know an inventor's name,
have you noticed that
it is often a White American?
For example, in a quiz
two answers could well be that
Alexander Graham Bell
invented the telephone
and Thomas Edison invented the electric light bulb.

Few people have heard of
Lewis Howard Latimer, the Black man
who actually invented the first light bulb
with a long enough life to be useful,
and who did the technical drawings
for ''Bell's'' telephone.

Latimer was not alone.
Black people have played a big part
in creating the modern world,
from medical techniques
like storing blood and heart surgery,
to inventing household things
which we take for granted.

F

So the next time you
change a light bulb,
make a phone call,
use an ironing board,
hear a clock chime,
put on make-up,
wear shoes made in a factory,
fill your car with oil,
stop at a red traffic light
or catch a train,
think of the forgotten scientists.
Some of their stories are in this book.
See under B, C, E, J, L, M, O, R, S, T and W.

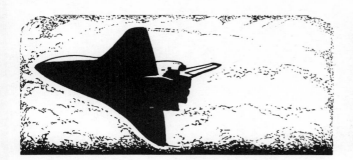

G

## Gillam

Since 1966, Isaac Gillam
has been in charge of
many of NASA's operations.
NASA runs America's space programme.
In 1976, Gillam became
Director of Shuttle Operations.
Until 1983, he was in charge of
approach and landing tests
for America's Space Shuttle.

G **Gourdine (1929 —      )**

Meredith Gourdine was born
in New Jersey, USA, in 1929.
In 1952 he won an Olympic Silver Medal
in the long jump.
In the early sixties, he raised money
to set up his own company, Gourdine Systems.
His aim was to make practical
an old way of getting a high voltage
from a low voltage source.
Using this method,
he has invented new ways
of paint-spraying, printing
and pollution control.
But perhaps we will soon hear more about
the most important part of his work,
which is a cheaper way
of supplying electricity to our homes,
direct from coal mines.

G

## Gregory

Only the very best aircraft pilots
become test pilots.
Frederick Gregory is not only a test pilot —
he tested the cockpit of the Space Shuttle.
He has also made a new model
of the Space Shuttle's cockpit.

One of his other inventions
is a ''single-handed'' controller.
This allows a pilot to control
with only one hand
the power, roll and tilt of an aircraft.

G

Gregory is also part of the team
that invented a new system
which allows aircraft to land
without the need of a human pilot.
This system makes it possible
for aircraft to land in thick fog,
under computer control.
It is now in use
at all major airports.

Gregory was expected to become
the first Black American in space,
but this honour went to
Guy Bluford, in August, 1983.

## Heart Pacemakers

Many people are alive and active today
because of the Heart Pacemaker.
A pacemaker keeps the heart beating regularly.
The operation to put in a pacemaker
is now done all over the world.
It is a proven method
of giving longer life to people
with some types of heart disease.

H

The man who invented the control unit
used in pacemakers is Otis Boykin,
a Black American.
He was born in Dallas in 1920.
In 1941 Boykin worked as a postal clerk,
but he later went on to university.
In all, he has invented more than 28 devices,
including one used in all guided missiles
and IBM computers.

Imhotep page 46

I

## Imes (b. 1893)

Elmer Samuel Imes, a Black American,
was a pioneer in Atomic Physics.
Without Dr. Imes' work (around 1919)
certain types of rocket engines
and chemical lasers
would not have been possible.
He played a great role
in expanding space sciences.

## Imhotep

Imhotep the Great was born in Ancient Egypt
in about 3000 BC,
in the city of Memphis.
His birthday was the 16th day of Epihi,
the third month of the harvest season,
which to us would be July.
His name means ''He who cometh in peace''.

He grew up to be
one of the greatest architects
the world has known.
His father, Kanofer, was also an architect.
Like father like son,
Imhotep followed in his father's footsteps.
He also became Pharaoh Zoser's Prime Minister.
Zoser was lucky to have such a clever man
for his chief adviser.

Imhotep spent a lot of time studying.
He was many other things too,
including the father of modern medicine.
He built the world's first hospital.
It is called the Temple of Imhotep
and it still stands today
on the island of Phile, in Egypt.
Nobles from all over the world
came to the Island of Phile
to be treated by Egyptian doctors.

The Greeks and the Persians
were the first outsiders
to find out how good the Egyptian doctors were.
Among their writings is
the ''Edwin Smith Papyrus'',
found in an Egyptian tomb,
which was mostly written by Imhotep.

Imhotep also studied maths and the stars
and designed the first step pyramid.
This led to the building
of the great pyramids.

Imhotep was Egypt's national hero.
He was a wise man,
the world's first multi-genius.
The Egyptians believed in life after death.
If a man was such a genius on earth
he was to be worshipped for ever.
When Imhotep died,
he was worshipped as a god,
just as Jesus became part of the Holy Trinity.

## Industrial Tools

The Egyptians had a variety of tools
for industrial work. For example,
they used a saw for woodwork
and a bow drill for drilling
holes for wooden nails.
They had another type of drill
for stone masonry.

Drawings of people at work with these tools
are found on the walls
of the pyramids and temples.
Some of the tools themselves
have been found by archaeologists.

The Egyptians used a lot of pottery.
Making pots was made easier
by using the potter's wheel
and by building kilns (ovens)
to bake the pottery.

## Iron Smelting

Two thousand years ago,
Africans on the West Bank of Lake Victoria
had a method of making carbon steel.
Very high temperatures are needed
to make carbon steel.
The method used in Africa so long ago
was better than any used in Europe
until a hundred years ago.
The African method also uses less fuel
and is so complex
that it looks more like the method
we now use to make computer micro-chips.

Remains of these steel-making furnaces
can be found in several areas
of Tanzania and Uganda.
People alive today still remember
every detail of how to make
and use these furnaces.

## Irrigation

The Ancient Egyptians
controlled the waters of the River Nile
and so controlled
the growing of their food.
They used a system of irrigation
(which means controlling water)
known as ''Basin Irrigation''.
This was because their fields
were divided into basins
by banks of earth.

The flood waters of the river
were brought to water the fields
by man-made dikes (ditches) and canals.
Small fruit trees were planted
on higher ground
and it is clear that
enough water was raised up
to water them.

There were many devices for lifting water.
The most basic is called a Serekh.
Then there is the Shadouf,
which is still in use today.
Later they had the "Eternal Screw".
It has been said that Archimedes,
a Greek scientist,
invented the Eternal Screw,
but, as we can see,
it was being used by Africans
three thousand years
before Archimedes was born,
in about 287 BC.

The same is true for
a lot of scientific knowledge
which, we are told, comes from Greece.
Why do historians teach us
that the knowledge comes from Greece,
when the Greeks themselves
said plainly that it came
from the Egyptians?

J

## Jones (1893 —     )

Where would we be without frozen foods?
Not only beef, lamb and chicken,
but all types of fruit and vegetables,
from all over the world;
things used daily in our homes?

The man who invented
the first portable system
that could keep things fresh
was Frederick McKinley Jones.

Jones did not have an easy start in life.
He had lost both parents by the age of ten.
He left school early
and worked as a labourer.
By the age of 16, he had learned enough
to get a job as a garage mechanic.
Three years later, he became garage foreman.

He later became interested in electronics
and designed a sound track system
for the local cinema.
This led to him getting a job
with a firm making sound equipment.
While in this job, he found out
that a lot of food was ruined
by the time it got to the shops —
because the ice to keep it cool had melted.
Before Jones' invention,
lorries and railway cars
had to be packed with ice
to keep foods fresh.
On average, a quarter of the food
would be ruined on arrival.

So, in 1949, using parts from the local scrapyard,
Jones designed the first practical
portable refrigeration system in the world.

In all, Jones invented more than 60 things,
among them the first portable X-ray machine.

## Just (1883-1941)

Ernest Just was known
as the ''scientist's scientist''
because he was so dedicated.
His subject was Biology.
He studied egg fertilization
and the structure of cells.
His first two years at college
were lonely and discouraging,
but he saw them through.
This Black boy from South Carolina
made himself one of the greatest scientists
in the early part of this century.

J

He was not interested
in awards and praise.
He just wanted to get on with his work.
In 1914 he even tried
to refuse a medal,
but it was given to him anyway.
Although he tried
to stay away from the limelight,
the news of his work
spread all over the world.
In all, he wrote two major books
and over sixty scientific papers.

K

## Khafare

Many people used to visit Ancient Egypt.
They came to see the doctors,
they came to study
or they came as tourists
to see the wonderful sights.
We know this because the foreign visitors
left graffiti on the walls of many buildings.
In the end, out of jealousy,
they came as enemies
to do battle with the Egyptians,
to take over their great achievements
and claim them as their own.

Pharaoh Khafare ordered the Great Sphinx
to be built at Giza.

**K** He had his bold African features
carved on the face of the Sphinx.
This is proof to the world
that the original Egyptians
were true Africans,
not Asians or Europeans,
as people might be led to think.

It is also said that
when Napoleon invaded Egypt in 1799,
he was so upset to see the face of an African
looking over the land
from the face of the Sphinx,
that he ordered his men
to blow off the face with a cannon.

## Khufu

The pyramids at Giza, in Egypt, are one
of the Seven Wonders of the World.
Not even a computer can decide
on a method to build one.
Plans for a pyramid were made
in Queen Victoria's time,
by British architects,
but work was never started.
So we can safely say that
Five thousand years ago, the Egyptians
were the world's greatest architects.

The largest and highest pyramid at Giza
is over 400ft high
and each side of the base is 755ft long.
Pharaoh Khufu's pyramid was the highest building
for five thousand years, until the skyscrapers
were built in America in the 1960's.

K

**K** In Ancient Egypt it was traditional
that as soon as the Pharaoh was crowned,
his subjects would start to build his tomb.
Khufu's pyramid probably took
about twenty-five years to build.

In Highgate Cemetery in London,
people have built tombs
like the Egyptian ones (but smaller!)
This part of the cemetery
is called the Egyptian Avenue.

## Latimer (1848-1928)

L

The very first electric light bulb
was invented by Thomas Edison.
But Edison's bulb had serious problems.
It burned out quickly
and was easily damaged.

Lewis Latimer, a Black American,
invented the first long-life bulb.
Latimer patented it in 1881.
Later, Edison asked Latimer
to join the team of inventors
known as ''The Edison Pioneers.''

Latimer was the son of runaway slaves.
He was in the Union Navy
during the American Civil War.
After the war,
he found it hard to get a job.

In the end, he found a job
as office boy in a small firm.
Then he bought his own tools
and taught himself to draw so well
that he soon became

L

a draughstman for the firm.

Not long after this,
Latimer became close friends
with Alexander Graham Bell.
Bell invented the telephone.
Latimer made the patent drawings
for the first telephone.

In 1879, Latimer met Herman Maxim,
who had invented the machine-gun.
Maxim was then the head
of an electric lighting company
and Latimer now learned
a lot more about electricity.

Two years later, he invented his light bulb
and afterwards wrote the first text-book
on electric lighting.

L

Maxim set up factories
to make some of Latimer's inventions.
Latimer was in charge of setting up
one of these factories in London.
He also set up street lighting
in New York and Montreal, Canada.

Latimer was a man of many parts —
inventor, draughtsman,
musician, poet and artist.
He was also active
in the Civil Rights Movement.

## Linen

L

The Ancient Egyptians were
one of the first to make linen.
They did this by growing
a plant called flax.
The flax was woven on a loom.
The threads were arranged
in different patterns
and dyed in different colours.

Experts say that
the quality of Ancient Egyptian cloth
is better than the best we have today.
What is more,
five thousand years later,
the same looms are used in modern-day Egypt.

McCoy page 67

## Mathematics

It is believed that the use of mathematics
started in parts of Asia.
But there are no buildings
as old as the pyramids
in Asia or the rest of the world.
Nor are there any maths books
as old as the ones found in Egypt.
From this we can say that the Ancient Egyptians
were the first great mathematicians.
They used addition, subtraction,
division, multiplication,
fractions, geometry and algebra.
They had a decimal system of numbers
with signs for one, ten, one hundred,
one thousand, ten thousand,
a hundred thousand and one million.

When they wrote a number,
each sign was repeated
as many times as it was needed.
**M** We know about these signs
because they were found
in the tombs of the Pharaohs.

The Ancient Egyptians used their maths
in architecture and technical drawing.
For example, plans for the pyramids
and temples have been found.
So has the original graph
for perhaps the most famous Egyptian
work of art — the Sphinx.

## McCoy (1843-1929)

Here comes the Real McCoy
with his invention.
He was born in Canada,
where his parents went
to escape from slavery.
As a young man
he was interested
in machines and tools.
He enjoyed watching them move.
He went back to America
after the Civil War,
when slavery was done away with.
He got a job in a machine shop,
where he got a chance to work on
the things he was obsessed with.
He set out to solve the problem
of how to oil machines
when they were moving.

M

Before McCoy, every machine had to be stopped
for oil to be put in,
to cut down on wear and tear.
This cost time and money.
McCoy invented the ''Drip-cup''
and 23 new lubricants.

**M** The first was patented in 1872.

His fame spread all over the world.
People used to ask
about the oil in a machine
''Is it the real McCoy?''
because his oils were so good.
Eager to get on, he produced two or three new
inventions every year —
for example, an ironing board and a lawn sprinkler,
as well as new brands of oil.
He started his own company
in Michigan
to sell his inventions.

M

He was so proud of his work,
he made people proud of him too.
He was a self-taught mechanic,
the son of a fugitive,
the Real McCoy.

## Moody (1882-1947)

Harold Moody was a doctor.
He started his own practice
in Peckham, South London, in 1913,
and was a local GP for many years,
well-loved for his kindness.

He came to Britain from Jamaica
at the age of 22
to study medicine at King's College Hospital.
British racism took him by surprise.
At first, he could not even find a room to rent.
As a student he won many prizes,
but was turned down for his first job at King's
because the matron refused to work
with a "coloured" doctor.

He was also turned down for a job
working with poor people in Camberwell,
because the employers said his White patients
"would not have a nigger attend them".
When he started his own practice
he earned less than a pound a week,
but he built it up to be very popular.

**M**

Dr. Moody never forgot
his early clashes with British racism.
Once he was successful,
he worked for the welfare
of other Black people in Britain
and, in 1931, he formed
the League of Coloured Peoples.
This was the first Black pressure group in Britain.
It supported Black people's rights
in housing and jobs
and took up cases of racism.

One success was in 1940
when the head of the BBC apologised
for the use of the word ''nigger''
in a radio programme.

M

During World War Two, the League helped
the thousands of Black skilled workers and soldiers
who came to work in factories
and fight in the armed forces.
The British Government was forced to state
''We fight this war ... for all peoples''.
It had to set up hostels for Black workers
and promise freedom for ''the colonies''
when the war was over.

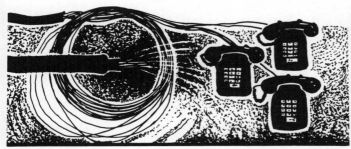

Northover page 76

## Navigation

It takes a lot of organisation
to build large ships.
How organised was African society
before Europeans went to Africa?

Did Africans build any boats
larger than the ones we have all seen
in Tarzan films?
Yes.
There were ships over 100 feet long
and over 14 feet wide.
They could carry over 120 people.

N

Did Africans do more than cross rivers
in these ships?
Yes.
They traded goods with each other,

**N** like rice, butter, metals,
cotton and beautiful garments.

Was this trade organised?
Yes.
We know of a fleet of 80 ships
each one with more than 80 tons in goods.

How far did these ships travel?
More than two and a half thousand miles
along the River Niger.

Did Africans go out to sea?
Yes.
The Chinese write
that Africans sailed to China
to trade elephants.
And, thanks to Professor Van Sertima and others,
we know that they went to America,
long before Columbus.

**N**

## Northover

William Northover is a chemist.
For the past thirty years
he has worked with glass.
His work has helped
to make things like transistors last longer.
He has also worked on glass fibres.
These are tubes of glass
used to carry information.
By passing light along a fibre,
we can have faster, cheaper
and more reliable telephone
and computer systems.
Three miles used to be the limit
that information could travel
along one length of fibre.
Northover has made glass fibres
that can carry information
for over ten miles.

N

## Open Heart Surgery

Daniel Hale Williams (1858-1931),
or ''Doctor Dan'', as he was known,
started his working life
as a shoemaker's apprentice.
He also worked on lake steamers
and as a barber
while he studied to achieve his ambition —
to be a doctor.
He graduated in Chicago in 1883.
At that time, there were no hospitals
for Black people in Chicago.
Operations were done at home
on the kitchen table or a couch.
Doctor Dan stopped this nonsense
by founding the Provident Hospital,
open to all races.

O

Here it was, in 1891,
that a young man was brought in
after a street-fight,
with a knife wound
in an artery right by his heart.
Williams sewed it up and the man lived.
This was the first successful
open heart surgery.

O

Williams was very active in the training
of Black doctors and nurses.
He was also active
in the work of the NAACP
(National Association for
the Advancement of Colored People).
This played an important part
in the Civil Rights Movement
from the early years of this century.
Many of the Black scientists in this book
**were awarded medals and prizes by the NAACP.**

Polar Exploration page 80

## Paper

The Ancient Egyptians were the first
to make paper. They used a plant
called the Papyrus plant.
The word 'paper' comes from 'Papyrus'.
The paper was made by stripping the plant
and laying the stems
in a criss-cross pattern.
This was then beaten together
for about an hour
and left in the sun to dry in its own juices.

Much of what we know
about the Egyptians' way of life
comes from papyrus books.
These books, found in temples and tombs
have lasted thousands of years.

P

## Polar Exploration

Matthew Henson, a Black man
was the first explorer
to reach the North Pole.
(We do not know
if the Eskimos got there first!)

Born in the USA, in 1866,
Henson became personal assistant
to Robert Peary at the age of 21.
Henson was an Able Seaman at the time
and Peary was a bold explorer.
Their first voyage was to Nicaragua, in 1887.
They first tried to reach the North Pole in 1891.
Eighteen years later, they finally made it.

The dangers that polar explorers
had to pass through
are impossible for us to understand.

P

Can we understand 65 degrees below zero,
in the open air, with the wind howling?
Or sleeping in ice huts,
with a floor made of ice?

For food there was only
hard pressed beef, stale biscuits,
tough dog meat and seal fat.

Clothing was a great problem.
If you tried to cover your face,
your skin would be peeled off
when you removed the covering.

P

Flying ice cost Henson an eye.
In eighteen years of exploration,
Peary lost nine of his toes
through stubbing them on the ice.
Cold toes simply break off.

About the 1894 and 1895 trips, Henson said,
''...The long race with death
across the 450 miles of the ice-cap
of North Greenland in 1895,
with Commander Peary and Hugh Lee,
are still the most vivid.''

Why did they do it?
Your guess is as good as mine.
Did it have any practical use?
Well, the area is rich
in oil, coal, gold and fish.
It also became a route
for air traffic.

On these trips
Henson was second-in-command.
He prepared everything
and designed a sledge
which was better than any of its time.

Henson's sledge is now on show
in the American Museum of Natural History,
in New York.

Their last trip began in 1908.
The best athletes were chosen,
but, one by one,
they broke down under the strain.
In the end, only Henson,
Peary and four Eskimos
made it to the North Pole.
Henson was the first to stand
on top of the world.
While Henson planted the flag of the USA,
Peary (having lost nine toes)
"sat exhausted on a sledge
and feebly waved his hand."

P

When they got back,
they had to spend two years
proving their claim.
Stupid questions were asked of Peary,
like why did he take a Black man
when there were so many Whites
to choose from?

P

The government gave Peary
the Congressional Medal of Honour
and made him an admiral.
Henson got nothing.
Later, some of his Black friends
gave him a gold watch
and some White businessmen
gave him a silver loving cup.

## Quarterman

Dr Quarterman was one of six Black scientists
in the team that made
the first atomic bomb, in 1945.
He was also in the group
that made the first nuclear reactor.

He is now retired,
after working for thirty years
with dangerous substances,
many of which he discovered himself.
During this time he worked with
many other well-known scientists,
including Albert Einstein.

He invented what is known as
"The Diamond Window", to be able to observe
Hydrogen Fluoride, which is one of
the most corrosive substances in the world.

Q | Dr Quarterman was also the first to work
on artificial blood.
"We live in the world of the unknown", he said.
"That's the only place to live."

## Railways

How could engines, coaches and wagons
be firmly linked into one train,
then taken apart to make up another train,
as and when needed?
Before the days of radio,
how could train drivers be told
when and where to stop
and about other traffic on the line?
In the early days of railways,
answers had to be found
for these questions. They were vital
for the running of the system
and the safety of passengers and staff.
Three Black Americans were responsible.

The next time you get on a train,
remember Andrew Beard,
inventor of the "Jenny Coupler".
This joined carriages
by just bumping them together
and was much safer
than coupling by hand.

R The other two inventors
were Garrett Morgan and Granville Woods.
Morgan invented traffic lights
and Woods the "Induction Telegraph".
This made it possible for moving trains
to be in contact with stations
and other trains on the line.

Both Morgan and Woods
invented many other things.
For example, Morgan invented the gas mask.
Woods invented an incubator, boiler and air-brake.
Both also had to fight
for the credit and the rewards
of their inventions.

Morgan, for instance,
had to take on White salesmen
to persuade his mainly White customers
to buy his gas masks.
And Woods at one point
had to go to court to prove
that he was the true inventor
of his telegraph.

R

### Rillieux (b. 1806)

Norbert Rillieux was from New Orleans,
in the American South.
He invented a new way to make sugar,
which transformed the industry.
Disgusted with American racism,
he went to France,
where the French Government
made him Head of the Central School.

When he died, the New Orleans papers
wrote columns about the city's famous son,
but they would not put in
the fact that he was Black.

R

Shipbuilding page 93

## Seacole (1805-1881)

Mary Seacole is truly a credit
to the medical profession.
Jamaican-born Mary took great care
of the sick and wounded.
She travelled a lot,
making people well wherever she went.

She played a heroic part
in the Crimean War (1853-'56),
when Britain fought Russia.
In the Crimea, now part of the USSR,
Mary opened a ''guest house''
for the sick and wounded.
This was at the same time
as Florence Nightingale,
whose name is better-known.
Mary did her work
even though the British Government
told her she was not needed.

**S**

After the war, she went to Britain.
She had used all her money
nursing the sick and wounded
and was bankrupt — but not for long.
Her friends wrote to The Times
and Punch Magazine
and soon money was sent in
by her old patients, royalty and the public.

We have her to thank
for her medicine to treat cholera,
a killer disease,
which she treated
in Central America, the Crimea
and the Caribbean.

Mary Seacole died on 14 May, 1881.
She gave her life
to the medical profession,
but it was only after her death
that she was given great honour.

## Shipbuilding

The Egyptians used the River Nile
as a highway for river traffic.
There were many kinds of ships and boats,
made of papyrus, rushes and reeds.
Later they were made of wood.
The oldest known ship
was built mainly of cedar wood.
It belonged to Pharaoh Khufu, the king
who also ordered the building
of the largest pyramid at Giza.
The ship was found near his pyramid
in the 1950's. It is 142 feet long.

S

Smaller boats used by the Egyptians
included canoes and rowing boats.
For safety on board,
they had lifebelts made of papyrus.
Flat-bottomed barges were used
to carry heavy cargo
such as building stones and large sculptures.
These were carried
straight from the quarries
on the cliffs of the Nile,
to the temples and cemeteries.

S

For sea voyages, there were
passenger and cargo ships.
Wickerwork cabins made long journeys
more pleasant for the passengers.

There was plenty of room for cargo,
because the Egyptians
did a lot of trading
all over the world.

The same was true for other parts of Africa.
Africans sailed in so many different craft,
from small boats to luxury ships,
complete with kitchens and cabins.
They went as far as the Middle East,
Asia, China and the Americas.
Many people would not believe this,
but Professor Van Sertima
shows it in his book
"They Came Before Columbus".

S

## Shoes

Jan Matzeliger (1852-1889),
invented the first machine
that could make an entire shoe.
It took him twelve years of hard work
to do what the experts
thought was impossible.
Many had tried and failed.
His machine was so complicated
that people could not believe their eyes.
Yet it could make a perfect shoe
in one minute.

S

Matzeliger was born in Dutch Guiana.
At eighteen, he left for America.
In Lynn, Massachusetts,
he worked in a shoe factory,
where it took time and a lot of skill
to make a shoe.

People really did laugh at his idea,
but in the end he had the last laugh.
At first, he used bits of wood
to make parts for his machine.
Later, he made metal parts
in a blacksmith's yard
that was no longer in use.

They called his invention
"The Niggerhead Machine."
Within five years,
nine out of every ten shoes
were made by his machine.
Lynn became the shoe capital of the world.
The price of shoes fell by half
and wages doubled.

S

Millions of dollars were made,
but not by Matzeliger.
Sadly, he died soon after from TB —
brought on by overwork.
He was only 37 years old.

S

## Telescopes

In school, we are told that
Galileo invented the telescope.
But Galileo, the great scientist,
said that the ancients had telescopes.
And, recently, lenses have been found in Africa
to support Galileo's claim.
Perhaps this is how the Dogon*
have learned so much about the stars.

Modern telescopes are electronic devices,
often costing a fortune to make.
The one used on the moon
by the Apollo 16 crew in 1972
was designed by Dr. George Carruthers,
a Black American.
It was the first telescope
to operate from the moon.

*Dogon: see under D.

T

Carruthers was born in Ohio in 1939.
At high school in Chicago,
his futuristic thinking was put down
by most of his teachers
and he was jeered at school science fairs.
Yet, by the age of 26,
he had applied for a patent
for his camera telescope.
Because of Carruthers' invention,
we now know more about
the Earth and its atmosphere,
the gas and dust in space,
how stars are formed —
and life on Mars!
It was indeed a giant leap forward.
As Astronaut John W. Young,
in charge of the moon landing, said,
"I think new knowledge
coming from astronomers like him
will revolutionise the way we think."

## Temple (1830-1854)

In 1986 the killing of whales for profit
was banned.
This was done to give the whale
a chance to survive.

It was a different story in 1830,
when John Lewis Temple was born, in the USA.
There were many more whales in the seas
and we were looking for
better ways of killing them.

T

Lewis Temple worked as a blacksmith
and a part of his skill
was making harpoons for whaling.

In 1848, the 18 year old Temple
invented a new type of harpoon.
When a whale was hit,
the shaft of this harpoon
would turn and lock in position
at right angles to the hook.

The result was that

| T |

twice as many whales were caught.
The harpoon was called ''The Temple Toggle''.
In 1926, it was described as
''... the most important single invention
in the whole history of whaling.''

## Universities

Africa was one of the first
civilised continents.
In particular,
the Africans in Ancient Egypt
were one of the world's first civilised peoples.
About five thousand years ago,
they had a body of knowledge
which was passed on
through a secret society,
called the Mystery System.
It took fifty years for a student
to learn all the knowledge.

U

At first they allowed only Africans
to study at their universities.
Later the Greeks and Persians
were allowed in, as long as they promised
not to write anything down
or claim the knowledge as their own.

This was the rule
of the Kemetic universities.
The Egyptians called themselves the Kemets,
which means "Black People".
"Egyptians" was a name
given to them by the Greeks.

U

## Van Sertima

Without the work of Ivan Van Sertima,
it would be much harder to find books
about Black people in science and technology
and many other parts of Black History.
A lot of our research for this book
started with reading his works.
Professor Van Sertima was born in Guyana
and now lives in the USA.

He studied in London,
at the School of Oriental and African Studies,
and comes to give lectures in Britain
about once a year.
His books and lectures inspire many people
to look for the real facts
behind the versions of history
written by many White historians.

**V**

His work is inspiring,
because he takes great care to back up
everything he says with facts.

Two of his books are
"They Came Before Columbus"
and "Blacks in Science".
His main point is that
Africa is the cradle of civilisation
and that Africans played the major role
in creating the science and technology
 that we know and use today.

### Walker (1869-1919)

Sarah Breedlove Walker, from Louisiana,
was orphaned at six.
Her first work was in a laundry.
She became a millionaire,
with a big house in New York,
by inventing "The Walker System" for hair,
and a range of beauty products.

The Walker System was a new and easy way
for Black women to style their hair.
Most Black people's hair has very tight curls.
"Madame Walker", as she was known,
invented a hair softener and comb
for those who wanted their hair straight.

**W**

She started her own company
to market her hair system,
and her own range of cosmetics.
It had over two thousand agents.

Her house in New York was famous
for its decorations, furniture
(including a gold-plated piano)
and Madame Walker's parties.

She also did a lot for charity
and did not forget her roots —
one of her donations set up
a girls' school in West Africa.

## Wright (1919 —     )

Jane Wright is one of the world's leading doctors
when it comes to treating cancer.
She is an expert in Chemotherapy.
This is a method in which
various drugs are used
to try to kill or slow down
the spread of the cancer.

In her home town of New York City,
Wright both studied and worked
at the New York Medical Centre.
In 1955, she became a Professor there
and the Director of Cancer Chemotherapy.
In 1967 she made history
by becoming the first Black Woman
to become Dean of a Medical School,
the very school
where she was herself a student.

W

She has also worked in Africa —
she once took a medical unit,
with the latest equipment and supplies,
including an X-Ray machine,
to country areas where the people
did not usually have access
to such treatment.

111

## The 'X' Group

The 'X' Group is another name
given to the Africans in Ancient Egypt.
It is also agreed that the 'X' Group
were the last African Pharaohs
before foreign invaders came.

X

European archaeologists agree
that these people were "negroid",
but refuse to call them Egyptians.
The Egyptians worked out many things
which are now vital parts
of modern science and technology.
The so-called 'X' Group
were the original Egyptians, and the
original Egyptians were true Africans.

X

## The 'Y' Poem

Why has this story never been told
when these great people lived in days of old?
Why has the truth been hidden for so long
about Imhotep, McCoy and the Dogon?
Africans like these and many more
have done plenty to even up the score.
Our people are worth their weight in gold
we are not useless as we have so often been told.
In science and technology it must be said
the evidence is here from A to Z.

Y

Y  Cowings, McCoy and Ancient Egyptians

Zodiac page 117

## Zimbabwe

The remains of this city-state
give us a glimpse
of the greatness of Africa
hundreds of years
before it was colonised.
Great Zimbabwe is also an outstanding example
of African stone architecture.

It was built more than
eight hundred years ago. At that time,
about ten thousand people lived there,
ruled by King Monomatapa.
His power was based
on mining gold and other metals
and he traded all over the world.

One end of the city is built on a hill.
This is known as the Royal Enclosure.
It was the king's official residence
and the place where treasures were kept.
Iron and copper were also smelted here.

At the other end, half a mile away,
is the Great Enclosure.
The wall of this enormous place
is a truly impressive sight.
It is 250 metres long
and is made up of
15 thousand tons of granite blocks.
It is 2 metres thick
and 10 metres high.

Great Zimbabwe is now a National Monument
which has given its name
to independent Zimbabwe.

Z

## Zodiac

Today some people never do anything
without reading their stars.
Some even go so far as
having their own personal chart written.
To have this done, you must know
the exact time and date of your birth.
This is so that the astrologer can check
to see the position
of the stars and planets
at the exact moment you were born.
Some people believe
that the changes in the heavens
go hand-in-hand with changes in your life.

Z

Seventeen thousand years ago in Africa
the Egyptians believed the same thing.
But it was not the newspapers
which advertised the horoscopes —
it was the priests who studied the stars.
Local people would make
daily visits to their priests
to find out about the movement of the stars
and how it would affect them.

For this and many other reasons
the African priest was very important
in the community.

Z

# Index

# E

# F

# G

# H

# List of Useful Books

They Came Before Columbus
Ivan Van Sertima

Blacks in Science
Ivan Van Sertima

Nile Valley Civilisations
Ivan Van Sertima

Great African Thinkers Vol 1 Cheikh Anta Diop
Ivan Van Sertima

African Origin of Civilisation: Myth or Reality
Cheikh Anta Diop

World's Great Men of Colour Vols 1 and 2
J.A. Rogers

Great Negroes Past and Present
Russell L. Adams

Wonderful Adventures of Mrs Seacole
Ziggi Alexander and Audrey Dewjee

Staying Power: The History of Black People in Britain
Peter Fryer


Most of these books are hard to find in the U.K.
Please contact The Bookplace for further information.
Telephone 01 701 1757

# Other Books ...

Please contact us for other books in this ALBSU-sponsored series for adult beginner readers, including:

■ **FOUR WOMEN by Frank Forde, Lesnah Hall, Virginia McLean and Ray Uter**
48 pages illustrated £1.00
ISBN 0906464 19 6

Life histories of Nanny of the Maroons, Sojourner Truth, Mary McLeod Bethune and Claudia Jones. The first in the Black Makers of History Series.

■ **THREE OR FIVE MINUTES by Betty Hammond**
32 pages illustrated 50p
ISBN 0906464 13 7

The first in the Fiction Series, about a woman, her family and a nuclear attack.

■ **A KIND OF LEAVING by Millie Richards**
32 pages colour photos £1.00
ISBN 0906464 23 4

The second in the Fiction Series, about a young Black Woman's struggle to find her own place to live.

■ **COCKNEY ADONIS by Kate Dowdall**
32 pages colour photos £1.00
ISBN 0906464 26 9

The third in the Fiction Series, about a love affair never to be forgotten.

Our bookshop also stocks a wide range of books, including a large Adult Basic Education section.

Write or phone for our catalogue of books from Peckham Publishing Project.

The Bookplace
13 Peckham High Street
London SE15 5EB
Tel: 01-701 1757